Johann Sebastian BACH

CHROMATIC FANTASIA & FUGUE IN D MINOR
for Two Clarinets in Bb and Bass Clarinet in Bb
J.S. BACH, BWV 903

Transcribed and Edited by Richard Stoltzman

SCORE

KEISER®

Performance notes

Breath marks are only suggestions. The length of time between breaths is not a contest. Varying the places in the music where you breathe is good to practice and allows for expressive use of the breath for spontaneous performances.

In the Fugue, *legato* groupings are simply suggestions for supple phrasing. Feel free to try alternative tonguing and legato combinations.

Remember that Bach did not indicate dynamics, breath marks, nuances or tempi in his scores. I use them to give some ideas for shaping the music. As you become more familiar with the piece through practice and performance, you will find your own path to communicate Bach's amazing music.

Recitativo (as it appears in the Fantasy) connotes a spoken style, less rhythmical in a particular tempo. Here, Bach is venturing through many harmonies to explore the descending chromatic half-step.

The last section of the Fantasy, which I marked *Adagio cantabile*, is a poignant dénouement unfolding of the chromatic scale, as only Bach, in his genius, can create. Two chromatic lines descend hand in hand. With stems up, we hear the melodic line finish each phrase: E-D# (m. 75), D-C#, C-B (m. 76), B-A#, A-G# (m. 77), and G-F#, F-E (m. 78). With grace notes stems down, we hear the top note of each chord (which I have indicated with a *tenuto* marking): A-G# (m. 75), G-F#-F-E (m. 76), E-D#-D-C# (m. 77), and C-B-A#-A (m. 78). Inspired art transcending craft.

In general, start trills from above on the upper auxiliary note.

➤ = Play the written note, then the note one step above and return to the main note.

➤ = Play the written note, then the note a step below and return to the main note.

Notes for the Accompanying Audio

The Chromatic Fantasia was recorded in a live performance at Minetsuku Hall in Nagoya, Japan 2010. Naturally, it is not perfect, but stands as my interpretation of this great music at that moment in time.

The Fugue was recorded in a studio in Boston 2008. Meghan Donahue Kerley played the Bass Clarinet part and I am on Clarinet 2. When you wish to play along with the audio, line up your audio player with the entrance of Clarinet 2, push pause, start the fugue and cue the sound at m. 9.

—Richard Stoltzman

*   *   *

All audio is available in the DOWNLOADS tab of www.keisersouthernmusic.com. You may either scan the tab manually or use the search field at the top right of the page. To download to your device, click on the desired audio link, then right-click on the play bar and select "Save Audio As..."

II. Fugue
for Two Clarinets in B♭ and Bass Clarinet in B♭

Transcribed and Edited by Richard Stoltzman

JOHANN SEBASTIAN BACH, BWV 903

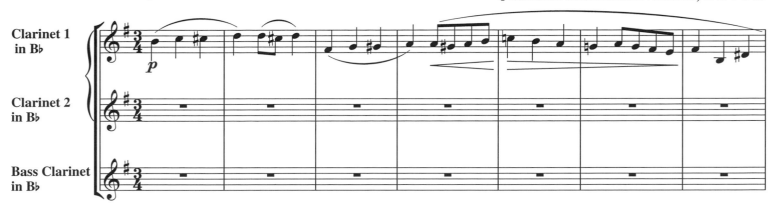

4

* ossia (alternative to Bass Clarinet part, mm. 53–56, if desirable)

* ossia (alternative to Bass Clarinet part, mm. 53–56, if desirable)

6

CHROMATIC FANTASIA
and FUGUE IN D MINOR
for Two Clarinets in B♭ and Bass Clarinet in B♭

Transcribed and Edited by Richard Stoltzman

JOHANN SEBASTIAN BACH, BWV 903

I. Fantasia
(Clarinet 1 solo)

2

Freely, with fantasy

Johann Sebastian BACH

CHROMATIC FANTASIA & FUGUE IN D MINOR
for Two Clarinets in Bb and Bass Clarinet in Bb
J.S. BACH, BWV 903

Transcribed and Edited by Richard Stoltzman

CLARINET II IN Bb

KEISER

II. Fugue

Clarinet 2 in B♭

* ossia (alternative to Bass Clarinet part, mm. 53–56, if desirable)

Johann Sebastian BACH

CHROMATIC FANTASIA & FUGUE IN D MINOR
for Two Clarinets in Bb and Bass Clarinet in Bb
J.S. BACH, BWV 903

Transcribed and Edited by Richard Stoltzman

Bass Clarinet in Bb

KEISER

II. Fugue

Bass Clarinet in B♭

* If low C-extension is available.

Performance notes

Breath marks are only suggestions. The length of time between breaths is not a contest. Varying the places in the music where you breathe is good to practice and allows for expressive use of the breath for spontaneous performances.

In the Fugue, *legato* groupings are simply suggestions for supple phrasing. Feel free to try alternative tonguing and legato combinations.

Remember that Bach did not indicate dynamics, breath marks, nuances or tempi in his scores. I use them to give some ideas for shaping the music. As you become more familiar with the piece through practice and performance, you will find your own path to communicate Bach's amazing music.

Recitativo (as it appears in the Fantasy) connotes a spoken style, less rhythmical in a particular tempo. Here, Bach is venturing through many harmonies to explore the descending chromatic half-step.

The last section of the Fantasy, which I marked *Adagio cantabile*, is a poignant dénouement unfolding of the chromatic scale, as only Bach, in his genius, can create. Two chromatic lines descend hand in hand. With stems up, we hear the melodic line finish each phrase: E-D♯ (m. 75), D-C♯, C-B (m. 76), B-A♯, A-G♯ (m. 77), and G-F♯, F-E (m. 78). With grace notes stems down, we hear the top note of each chord (which I have indicated with a *tenuto* marking): A-G♯ (m. 75), G-F♯-F-E (m. 76), E-D♯-D-C♯ (m. 77), and C-B-A♯-A (m. 78). Inspired art transcending craft.

In general, start trills from above on the upper auxiliary note.

∿ = Play the written note, then the note one step above and return to the main note.

∿ = Play the written note, then the note a step below and return to the main note.

Notes for the Accompanying Audio

The Chromatic Fantasia was recorded in a live performance at Minetsuku Hall in Nagoya, Japan 2010. Naturally, it is not perfect, but stands as my interpretation of this great music at that moment in time.

The Fugue was recorded in a studio in Boston 2008. Meghan Donahue Kerley played the Bass Clarinet part and I am on Clarinet 2. When you wish to play along with the audio, line up your audio player with the entrance of Clarinet 2, push pause, start the fugue and cue the sound at m. 9.

—Richard Stoltzman

*   *   *

All audio is available in the DOWNLOADS tab of www.keisersouthernmusic.com. You may either scan the tab manually or use the search field at the top right of the page. To download to your device, click on the desired audio link, then right-click on the play bar and select "Save Audio As..."

Performance notes

Breath marks are only suggestions. The length of time between breaths is not a contest. Varying the places in the music where you breathe is good to practice and allows for expressive use of the breath for spontaneous performances.

In the Fugue, *legato* groupings are simply suggestions for supple phrasing. Feel free to try alternative tonguing and legato combinations.

Remember that Bach did not indicate dynamics, breath marks, nuances or tempi in his scores. I use them to give some ideas for shaping the music. As you become more familiar with the piece through practice and performance, you will find your own path to communicate Bach's amazing music.

Recitativo (as it appears in the Fantasy) connotes a spoken style, less rhythmical in a particular tempo. Here, Bach is venturing through many harmonies to explore the descending chromatic half-step.

The last section of the Fantasy, which I marked *Adagio cantabile*, is a poignant dénouement unfolding of the chromatic scale, as only Bach, in his genius, can create. Two chromatic lines descend hand in hand. With stems up, we hear the melodic line finish each phrase: E-D# (m. 75), D-C#, C-B (m. 76), B-A#, A-G# (m. 77), and G-F#, F-E (m. 78). With grace notes stems down, we hear the top note of each chord (which I have indicated with a *tenuto* marking): A-G# (m. 75), G-F#-F-E (m. 76), E-D#-D-C# (m. 77), and C-B-A#-A (m. 78). Inspired art transcending craft.

In general, start trills from above on the upper auxiliary note.

= Play the written note, then the note one step above and return to the main note.

= Play the written note, then the note a step below and return to the main note.

Notes for the Accompanying Audio

The Chromatic Fantasia was recorded in a live performance at Minetsuku Hall in Nagoya, Japan 2010. Naturally, it is not perfect, but stands as my interpretation of this great music at that moment in time.

The Fugue was recorded in a studio in Boston 2008. Meghan Donahue Kerley played the Bass Clarinet part and I am on Clarinet 2. When you wish to play along with the audio, line up your audio player with the entrance of Clarinet 2, push pause, start the fugue and cue the sound at m. 9.

—Richard Stoltzman

*   *   *

All audio is available in the DOWNLOADS tab of www.keisersouthernmusic.com. You may either scan the tab manually or use the search field at the top right of the page. To download to your device, click on the desired audio link, then right-click on the play bar and select "Save Audio As…"

This page left intentionally blank for convenience of page turns.

Clarinet 1 in B♭

Performance notes

Breath marks are only suggestions. The length of time between breaths is not a contest. Varying the places in the music where you breathe is good to practice and allows for expressive use of the breath for spontaneous performances.

In the Fugue, *legato* groupings are simply suggestions for supple phrasing. Feel free to try alternative tonguing and legato combinations.

Remember that Bach did not indicate dynamics, breath marks, nuances or tempi in his scores. I use them to give some ideas for shaping the music. As you become more familiar with the piece through practice and performance, you will find your own path to communicate Bach's amazing music.

Recitativo (as it appears in the Fantasy) connotes a spoken style, less rhythmical in a particular tempo. Here, Bach is venturing through many harmonies to explore the descending chromatic half-step.

The last section of the Fantasy, which I marked *Adagio cantabile*, is a poignant dénouement unfolding of the chromatic scale, as only Bach, in his genius, can create. Two chromatic lines descend hand in hand. With stems up, we hear the melodic line finish each phrase: E-D# (m. 75), D-C#, C-B (m. 76), B-A#, A-G# (m. 77), and G-F#, F-E (m. 78). With grace notes stems down, we hear the top note of each chord (which I have indicated with a *tenuto* marking): A-G# (m. 75), G-F#-F-E (m. 76), E-D#-D-C# (m. 77), and C-B-A#-A (m. 78). Inspired art transcending craft.

In general, start trills from above on the upper auxiliary note.

~~~ = Play the written note, then the note one step above and return to the main note.

~~~ = Play the written note, then the note a step below and return to the main note.

Notes for the Accompanying Audio

The Chromatic Fantasia was recorded in a live performance at Minetsuku Hall in Nagoya, Japan 2010. Naturally, it is not perfect, but stands as my interpretation of this great music at that moment in time.

The Fugue was recorded in a studio in Boston 2008. Meghan Donahue Kerley played the Bass Clarinet part and I am on Clarinet 2. When you wish to play along with the audio, line up your audio player with the entrance of Clarinet 2, push pause, start the fugue and cue the sound at m. 9.

—Richard Stoltzman

*   *   *

All audio is available in the DOWNLOADS tab of www.keisersouthernmusic.com. You may either scan the tab manually or use the search field at the top right of the page. To download to your device, click on the desired audio link, then right-click on the play bar and select "Save Audio As..."

poco a poco dim.

poco a poco dim.

cresc. molto

10

Richard Stolzman
21st Century Series for Clarinet

R ichard Stoltzman's virtuosity, musicianship and sheer personal magnetism have made him one of today's most sought-after concert artists. As soloist with more than a hundred orchestras, as a captivating recitalist and chamber music performer, as an innovative jazz artist, and as a prolific recording artist, two-time Grammy Award winner Stoltzman has defied categorization, dazzling critics and audiences alike throughout many musical genres. *"His mastery of the clarinet and his impeccable musicianship are no secret by now, but one who has not heard him play for a time can easily forget how rich and fluid the instrument can sound from top to bottom of its range. If Mr. Stoltzman is not one of a kind, who might the others be?"* - **The New York Times**

SCHUBERT SONATINES 1 & 2, OPUS 137 FOR CLARINET AND PIANO WITH CD Stolztman, called the "greatest clarinetist in the world" by the Boston Globe, has transcribed and edited two Schubert Sonatines originally written for Violin, Op. posth. 137 for the clarinet. These two brilliant Sonatines, No. 1 in D (D384) and No. 2 in a minor (D385) are expertly engraved, formatted and set in a lovely edition with high quality paper. Both Sonatines are available in one folio. Sonatine No. 1 is transcribed for Clarinet in A and No. 2 for Bb Clarinet. Mr. Stoltzman provides insights and performance suggestions in this classic edition.

HLC00042593.. $22.95

BACH CHROMATIC FANTASIA AND FUGUE IN D MINOR WITH CD This masterly and sublime classic J. S. Bach work has been expertly transcribed and arranged for three clarinets that begins with a solo clarinet tour de force edited by world class artist Richard Stoltzman. The CD recording provides performance insights to the Fantasia and accompaniment for the Fugue. Now clarinetists can play this masterwork in a setting created by one of the world's greatest clarinet players. This edition encompasses expert music engraving and quality paper and printing. It should be in every clarinet player's library for a lifetime of enjoyment and admiration.

HLC00042681 ....$19.95

BRAHMS INTERMEZZO OP. 118, NO. 2 In the span of three years, Brahms composed a veritable treasure trove of clarinet music. First came the Trio, Op. 114, which was followed in the same year by the Quintet, Op. 115 (1891). Then, in 1894 he gave us his Sonatas: Op. 120 No. 1 &2. Nestled amidst these fervid works is the melancholy Intermezzo, Op. 118 No. 2 (1893). Though written for the piano, one can easily imagine the memory of Richard Mühfeld, Brahms' "nightengale" of the clarinet, haunting the melodic lines which seem to flow so effortlessly. In this transcription of Brahms' Intermezzo from his "Six Pieces for Piano", Op. 118,. the clarinetist may choose to perform in the original key of A, with parts provided for A and B-flat clarinets; or in an alternate version in B-flat (includes transposed piano score and B-flat clarinet part).

HLC00046282... $9.95